> RECIPE OF THE WEEK

BURGERS

RECIPE OF THE WEEK

BURGERS

52 EASY RECIPES FOR YEAR-ROUND COOKING

SALLY SAMPSON

PHOTOGRAPHY BY YUNHEE KIM

WILEY

JOHN WILEY & SONS, INC.

Copyright © 2008 by Sally Sampson. All rights reserved

Published by John Wiley & Sons, Inc., Hoboken, New Jersey

Published simultaneously in Canada

For general information about our other products and services, please contact our Customer Care Department within the United States at (800) 762-2974, outside the United States at (317) 572-3993 or fax (317) 572-4002. Wiley also publishes its books in a variety of electronic formats. Some content that appears in print may not be available in electronic books. For more information about Wiley products, visit our web site at www.wiley.com.

BOOK DESIGN BY DEBORAH KERNER

PHOTOGRAPHY COPYRIGHT © 2008 BY YUNHEE KIM

FOOD STYLING BY JEE LEVIN

PROP STYLING BY LYNN BUTLER BELING

Library of Congress Cataloging-in-Publication Data:

Sampson, Sally, 1955-
    Recipe of the week : burgers / Sally Sampson ; photography by Yunhee Kim.
        p. cm.
    Includes index.
    ISBN 978-0-470-16944-5 (pbk. : alk. paper)
    1. Cookery (Meat) 2. Hamburgers. I. Title. II. Title: Burgers.
    TX749.5.B43S36 2008
    641.6′6—dc22

                        2007027376

Printed in China

10 9 8 7 6 5 4 3 2 1

Acknowledgments

⬤ ⬤ ⬤ ⬤ ⬤ ⬤ ⬤ ⬤ ⬤ ⬤

Love and appreciation to Lauren and Ben, first of all and most of all. And to Carla and Justin, who make everything happen.

Contents

introduction

When I started this book, I hadn't given much thought to the history of the burger. In fact, I hadn't given it any thought at all. But when friends found out what I was doing, I was barraged with questions about **the genesis** of the name and of the burger itself. As with other popular foods, countless countries, people and eateries have clamored for credit. Among them: Genghis Khan; his grandson Kublai Khan; German sailors; meat choppers in New York; meat choppers in Los Angeles; Charlie Nagreen from Wisconsin; Charlie Menches from Akron, Ohio; Oscar Bilby from Tulsa, Oklahoma; Louis Lassen from New Haven, Connecticut; Fletch Davis from Athens, Texas; Walter Anderson from Wichita, Kansas; and even Popeye, the sailor man. McDonald's, In-N-Out Burger, Burger King and Wendy's all came much later and none claim to have invented the burger. Perfected, perhaps. Popularized, yes.

Like great art, **burgers were a natural idea** that sprung up independently all over the world. And in the end, although most countries have their own versions, there are few foods, save apple pie, that are quite so completely and **thoroughly American**. My preference for meat is ground chuck, 80 to 85% lean, but this is really a matter of taste. **My foolproof instructions to make the best burgers:**

Form the meat into ¾- to 1-inch-thick patties. Using your thumb or the back of a spoon, make a half-inch indentation about the size of a quarter in the center. If you don't indent the beef, you will get burgers with a bulge in the middle. Handle the patties as little as possible; do not work more than necessary.

Tips on Grilling

I grew up in New York City with a mother who regularly cooked great hamburgers on a cast iron skillet—with a mere sprinkling of salt on the bottom of the pan—and while I still love to cook them that same way, now that I have a porch and a backyard, I almost always use a grill instead.

The best way to grill is to invest in a chimney starter, available at most housewares and hardware stores. Simply fill the bottom with two pieces of crumpled newspaper and the top with hardwood lump charcoal. Light the newspaper and burn until the coals are glowing red, about 15 to 20 minutes. Dump the coals out into the bottom of the grill and, using tongs, spread them out evenly. Cover with the grate.

After five minutes, use a wire brush to thoroughly clean the grate. When the coals are covered with a pale gray ash and you can leave your hand five inches above the fire for three to four seconds, the coals are medium high and are ready for grilling!

the recipes

Classic Burgers with Homemade Tomato Ketchup

While I am not a huge fan of most store-bought ketchup, I love this homemade version. I especially like it left chunky.

FOR THE HOMEMADE TOMATO KETCHUP:

1 Spanish onion, chopped

2 tablespoons olive oil

One 28-ounce can whole tomatoes,
    including the puree

¼ cup cider vinegar

2 tablespoons brown sugar

1 tablespoon tomato paste

½ teaspoon kosher salt

½ teaspoon freshly ground black pepper

¼ teaspoon ground cinnamon

⅛ teaspoon ground allspice

FOR THE BURGERS:

1½ to 1¾ pounds ground chuck

1 teaspoon kosher salt

½ to 1 teaspoon freshly ground black
    pepper

To make the ketchup: Place a large skillet over medium-high heat and when it is hot, add the onion and cook, stirring, until soft and golden, 7 to 10 minutes. Add the remaining ketchup ingredients, reduce the heat to low and cook, stirring occasionally, until very thick, about 35 minutes. Set aside to cool. If you want a chunky ketchup, cover and refrigerate. For smooth, transfer to a food processor fitted with a steel blade and process to the desired texture. Cover and refrigerate at least overnight and up to 3 weeks. (Yield: about 2 cups)

To make the burgers: Place the beef on a work surface and divide into 4 balls of equal size. Form each into a patty about ¾ to 1 inch thick by tossing it back and forth between your hands. To ensure more even cooking, make a ½-inch indentation with your thumb in the center of the burger. Handle the patties as little as possible; do not work more than necessary.

Prepare a grill to medium-high. When the coals are glowing red, after 15 to 20 minutes, cover with the grate. After 5 minutes, use a wire brush to thoroughly clean the

grate. Brush the grate with oil. When the coals are covered with pale gray ash and you can leave your hand 5 inches above the fire for 2 to 3 seconds, the coals are ready.

Sprinkle both sides of the burgers with the salt and pepper. Place the burgers on the grate and grill until well seared on both sides, about 5 minutes for medium rare or 6 minutes for medium. Transfer to buns or a serving platter and serve immediately.

Alternatively, place a cast iron skillet over high heat and when it is hot but not smoking add the burgers to the dry pan. Cook until well seared on both sides, 8 to 10 minutes for medium rare or 10 to 12 minutes for medium.

Cognac and Chive Burgers

Simple but very sophisticated.

1½ to 1¾ pounds ground chuck

3 garlic cloves, unpeeled

2 tablespoons minced fresh chives

1 teaspoon cognac

1 teaspoon kosher salt

½ teaspoon freshly ground black pepper

Place the beef, garlic, chives and cognac in a large bowl and, using your hands, mix until the ingredients are evenly incorporated. Place the mixture on a work surface and divide into 4 balls of equal size. Form each into a patty about ¾ to 1 inch thick, tossing it back and forth between your hands. To ensure more even cooking, make a ½-inch indentation with your thumb in the center of the burger. Handle the patties as little as possible; do not work more than necessary.

Prepare a grill to medium-high. When the coals are glowing red, after 15 to 20 minutes, cover with the grate. After 5 minutes, use a wire brush to thoroughly clean the grate. Brush the grate with oil. When the coals are covered with pale gray ash and you can leave your hand 5 inches above the fire for 2 to 3 seconds, the coals are ready.

Sprinkle both sides of the burgers with the salt and pepper. Place the burgers on the grate and grill until well seared on both sides, about 5 minutes for medium rare or 6 minutes for medium. Transfer to buns or a serving platter and serve immediately.

Alternatively, place a cast iron skillet over high heat and when it is hot but not smoking add the burgers to the dry pan. Cook until well seared on both sides, 8 to 10 minutes for medium rare or 10 to 12 minutes for medium.

Curried Crab Cake Burgers

These are smaller and a bit more delicate than the other burgers made from fish so treat them gently. They also make great appetizers: just make them even smaller and serve one per person.

12 ounces crabmeat, very coarsely
　　shredded

½ cup panko breadcrumbs

¼ cup mayonnaise or whole milk yogurt

2 tablespoons chopped fresh cilantro leaves

1 tablespoon chopped fresh chives

1½ teaspoons curry powder

¼ cup all purpose flour

1 teaspoon kosher salt

2 tablespoons olive oil

1 lime, quartered

Place the crabmeat, panko, mayonnaise, cilantro, chives and curry powder in a medium-size bowl and, using your hands, mix very gently to combine. Form into 4 patties, cover and refrigerate for at least 1 hour and up to 4 hours.

Place the flour and salt on a large plate. Dredge each patty in the flour mixture. Place a large skillet over medium-high heat and when it is hot, add the oil. Add the patties and cook until lightly browned, about 4 minutes on each side. Serve immediately with the lime wedges.

Cheddar, Artichoke and Mushroom Burgers

I used to insist that artichokes only be eaten fresh but found that this significantly reduced my artichoke eating. Now that I have discovered frozen artichokes, I always keep at least two bags in my freezer. Almost all American artichokes are grown in California, mostly in Castroville, the Artichoke Center of the World.

1½ to 1¾ pounds ground chuck

½ cup chopped thawed, frozen artichokes

½ cup chopped button mushrooms

2 garlic cloves or 4 caramelized garlic cloves (page 9), finely chopped

1 teaspoon Dijon mustard

¼ pound cheddar cheese, grated

1 teaspoon kosher salt

½ to 1 teaspoon freshly ground black pepper

Place the beef, artichokes, mushrooms, garlic and mustard in a large bowl and, using your hands, mix until the ingredients are evenly incorporated. Place the mixture on a work surface and divide into 4 balls of equal size. Divide the cheddar cheese into 4 portions. Using your thumb or the back of a tablespoon, make a shallow hole in each portion of beef and fill it with cheese. Shape the burger and carefully seal the opening. Form each into a patty about ¾ to 1 inch thick, tossing it back and forth between your hands. To ensure more even cooking, make a ½-inch indentation with your thumb in the center of the burger. Handle the patties as little as possible; do not work more than necessary.

Prepare a grill to medium-high. When the coals are glowing red, after 15 to 20 minutes, cover with the grate. After 5 minutes, use a wire brush to thoroughly clean the grate. Brush the grate with oil. When the coals are covered with pale gray ash and you can leave your hand 5 inches above the fire for 2 to 3 seconds, the coals are ready.

Sprinkle both sides of the burgers with the salt and pepper. Place the burgers on the grate and grill until well seared on both sides, about 5 minutes for medium rare or 6 minutes for medium. Transfer to buns or a serving platter and serve immediately.

Alternatively, place a cast iron skillet over high heat and when it is hot but not smoking, add the burgers to the dry pan. Cook until well seared on both sides, 8 to 10 minutes for medium rare or 10 to 12 minutes for medium.

Caramelized Garlic Cloves

2 tablespoons olive oil

1 head garlic, separated and papery skin removed
   from cloves

Place a small pan over low heat and when it is hot, add the oil. Add the garlic and cook, stirring occasionally, until the garlic is softened and golden in color, about 20 minutes. Set aside to cool. Cover and refrigerate up to two weeks.

Jerk Burgers

When I first discovered Jamaican Jerk chicken, I made it at least three times a week. The original technique called for spicing and tenderizing the meat by poking it with holes which were then filled with spices. Today we no longer need to do that to achieve a smoky spicy flavor that I find irresistible.

1¼ to 1½ pounds ground turkey or chicken (1 package)

3 scallions, both white and green parts, coarsely chopped

1 tablespoon coarsely chopped jalapeño pepper or Scotch bonnet pepper

3 garlic cloves, minced

2 teaspoons soy sauce

1½ teaspoons Chinese five spice powder

1 teaspoon kosher salt, plus ½ teaspoon for sprinkling

1 teaspoon freshly ground black pepper, plus ½ teaspoon for sprinkling

¾ teaspoon allspice

½ teaspoon dried thyme

½ teaspoon ground nutmeg

1 lime, quartered

Place the turkey, scallions, jalapeño, garlic, soy sauce, five spice powder, salt, pepper, allspice, thyme and nutmeg in a large bowl and, using your hands, mix until the ingredients are evenly incorporated. Place the mixture on a work surface and divide into 4 balls of equal size. Form each into a patty about ¾ to 1 inch thick, tossing it back and forth between your hands. Handle the patties as little as possible; do not work more than necessary.

Prepare a grill to medium-high. When the coals are glowing red, after 15 to 20 minutes, cover with the grate. After 5 minutes, use a wire brush to thoroughly clean the grate. Brush the grate with oil. When the coals are covered with pale gray ash and you can leave your hand 5 inches above the fire for 2 to 3 seconds, the coals are ready.

Sprinkle both sides of the burgers with salt and pepper. Place the burgers on the grate and grill until well seared on both sides, about 5 minutes for medium rare or 6 minutes for medium. Transfer to buns or a serving platter and serve immediately with lime quarters.

Alternatively, place a cast iron skillet over high heat and when it is hot but not smoking add the burgers to the dry pan. Cook until well seared on both sides, 8 to 10 minutes for medium rare or 10 to 12 minutes for medium.

Curried Chicken Burgers with Chutney Mayonnaise

I have used this combination of classic Indian flavors on roast beef sandwiches, crab cakes, tuna sandwiches and salmon. I haven't yet found it to be a failure even in the most unusual settings.

FOR THE CHUTNEY MAYONNAISE:

2 tablespoons mayonnaise

2 tablespoons mango chutney

FOR THE BURGERS:

1¼ to 1½ pounds ground chicken or turkey
   (1 package)

¼ cup finely chopped fresh cilantro leaves,
   plus extra for garnish (optional)

1 tablespoon plus 1 teaspoon curry powder

1 tablespoon plus 1 teaspoon coconut, toasted
   or not, plus extra for garnish (optional)

2 teaspoons grated lime zest

1 teaspoon kosher salt

½ teaspoon freshly ground
   black pepper

To make the chutney mayonnaise: Place the mayonnaise and chutney in a small bowl and mix until well combined. Cover and refrigerate for at least 1 hour and up to 1 week.

To make the burgers: Place the chicken, cilantro, curry, coconut and lime zest in a large bowl and, using your hands, mix until the ingredients are evenly incorporated. Place the mixture on a work surface and divide into 4 balls of equal size. Form each into a patty about ¾ to 1 inch thick, tossing it back and forth between your hands. Handle the patties as little as possible; do not work more than necessary.

Prepare a grill to medium-high. When the coals are glowing red, after 15 to 20 minutes, cover with the grate. After 5 minutes, use a wire brush to thoroughly clean the grate. Brush the grate with oil. When the coals are covered with pale gray ash and you can leave your hand 5 inches above the fire for 2 to 3 seconds, the coals are ready.

continued on page 14

Sprinkle both sides of the burgers with the salt and pepper. Place the burgers on the grate and grill until well seared on both sides, about 5 minutes for medium rare or 6 minutes for medium. Transfer to buns or a serving platter and serve immediately topped with the chutney mayonnaise. Top with extra cilantro and coconut, if desired.

Alternatively, place a cast iron skillet over high heat and when it is hot but not smoking, add the burgers to the dry pan. Cook until well seared on both sides, 8 to 10 minutes for medium rare or 10 to 12 minutes for medium.

Steak Tartare Burgers

The inspiration for this fully cooked burger is steak tartare (or in Switzerland, Filet Américain), the classic raw dish of ground beef, onion, garlic, capers and other seasonings (originally with the now-banned raw egg). Legend has it that this dish originated with the Tartars, a Nomadic tribe who didn't have time to cook their meat. In order to stay true, serve these burgers on toast rather than on buns.

1½ to 1¾ pounds ground chuck

1 small red onion, halved and finely chopped (about 1 cup)

2 garlic cloves, finely chopped

¼ cup finely chopped fresh herbs, including parsley, cilantro and basil

1 tablespoon capers, drained and chopped

1 tablespoon Worcestershire sauce

1½ teaspoons Dijon mustard

1 teaspoon Tabasco

Juice and grated zest of 1 lemon

1 teaspoon kosher salt

½ teaspoon freshly ground black pepper

Place the beef, onion, garlic, herbs, capers, Worcestershire sauce, mustard, Tabasco, lemon juice and zest in a large mixing bowl and, using your hands, gently mix until the ingredients are evenly incorporated.

Place the beef on a work surface and divide into 4 balls of equal size. Form each into a patty about ¾ to 1 inch thick, tossing it back and forth between your hands. To ensure more even cooking, make a ½-inch indentation with your thumb in the center of the burger. Handle the patties as little as possible; do not work more than necessary.

Prepare a grill to medium-high. When the coals are glowing red, after 15 to 20 minutes, cover with the grate. After 5 minutes, use a wire brush to thoroughly clean the grate. Brush the grate with oil. When the coals are covered with pale gray ash and you can leave your hand 5 inches above the fire for 2 to 3 seconds, the coals are ready.

continued on next page

Sprinkle both sides of the burgers with the salt and pepper. Place the burgers on the grate and grill until well seared on both sides, about 5 minutes for medium rare or 6 minutes for medium. Transfer to toasted bread or a serving platter and serve immediately.

Alternatively, place a cast iron skillet over high heat and when it is hot but not smoking add the burgers to the dry pan. Cook until well seared on both sides, 8 to 10 minutes for medium rare or 10 to 12 minutes for medium.

Pork Burgers
with Fennel au Poivre

Traditionally, *au poivre* refers to a steak that is studded with ground pepper. The addition of the fennel slightly softens the zing of the pepper. I love to serve these burgers with a bitter green salad filled with apples, which contrasts nicely with the pork and fennel.

3 tablespoons coarsely ground black pepper

1 heaping tablespoon dried fennel

1 tablespoon finely chopped fresh
   rosemary leaves

1½ teaspoons kosher salt

1½ to 1¾ pounds ground pork

1 lemon, quartered

Place the pepper, fennel, rosemary and salt on a large plate and mix well. Place the ground pork on a work surface and divide into 4 balls of equal size. Dredge in the pepper mixture and form each ball into a patty about ¾ to 1 inch thick, tossing it back and forth between your hands. Handle the patties as little as possible; do not work more than necessary.

Prepare a grill to medium-high. When the coals are glowing red, after 15 to 20 minutes, cover with the grate. After 5 minutes, use a wire brush to thoroughly clean the grate. Brush the grate with oil. When the coals are covered with pale gray ash and you can leave your hand 5 inches above the fire for 2 to 3 seconds, the coals are ready.

Place the burgers on the grate and grill until well seared on both sides, about 5 minutes for medium rare or 6 minutes for medium. Transfer to buns or a serving platter and serve immediately, garnished with the lemon quarters.

Alternatively, place a cast iron skillet over high heat and when it is hot but not smoking add the burgers to the dry pan. Cook until well seared on both sides, 8 to 10 minutes for medium rare or 10 to 12 minutes for medium.

Lamb Burgers with Dates and Walnuts

The best dates to use for these burgers are chopped into little pieces and dredged in flour, usually oat flour. This helps prevent the dates from sticking together.

1½ to 1¾ pounds ground lamb

⅓ cup chopped dates

½ cup finely chopped walnuts

¼ cup pomegranate molasses

2 tablespoons chopped fresh chives

1 teaspoon kosher salt

½ teaspoon freshly ground black pepper

Thickened yogurt (page 58)

1 lemon, quartered

Place the lamb, dates, walnuts, molasses and chives in a large bowl and, using your hands, mix until the ingredients are evenly incorporated. Place the mixture on a work surface and divide into 4 balls of equal size. Form each into a patty about ¾ to 1 inch thick, tossing it back and forth between your hands. Handle the patties as little as possible; do not work more than necessary.

Prepare a grill to medium-high. When the coals are glowing red, after 15 to 20 minutes, cover with the grate. After 5 minutes, use a wire brush to thoroughly clean the grate. Brush the grate with oil. When the coals are covered with pale gray ash and you can leave your hand 5 inches above the fire for 2 to 3 seconds, the coals are ready.

Sprinkle both sides of the burgers with the salt and pepper. Place the burgers on the grate and grill until well seared on both sides, about 4 minutes for medium rare or 5 minutes for medium. Transfer to pita bread halves or a serving platter and serve immediately with thickened yogurt and/or the lemon quarters.

Alternatively, place a cast iron skillet over high heat and when it is hot but not smoking add the burgers to the dry pan. Cook until well seared on both sides, 8 to 10 minutes.

Chicken Burger with Black Olives and Caramelized Onions

MAKES 4 BURGERS

Although sage is considered a pungent and herby herb, when used in moderation (as it is here) I especially like it: it perfectly balances out the richness of the caramelized onions and the olives.

1¼ to 1½ pounds ground chicken or turkey (1 package)

½ cup chopped caramelized onions (page 29), plus additional for serving

¼ scant cup finely chopped black kalamata olives

1 teaspoon finely chopped fresh sage leaves (about 5)

1 teaspoon Hungarian paprika

1 teaspoon kosher salt

½ teaspoon freshly ground black pepper

Place the chicken, onions, olives, sage and paprika in a large bowl and, using your hands, mix until the ingredients are evenly incorporated. Place the mixture on a work surface and divide into 4 balls of equal size. Form each into a patty about ¾ to 1 inch thick, tossing it back and forth between your hands. Handle the patties as little as possible; do not work more than necessary.

Prepare a grill to medium-high. When the coals are glowing red, after 15 to 20 minutes, cover with the grate. After 5 minutes, use a wire brush to thoroughly clean the grate. Brush the grate with oil. When the coals are covered with pale gray ash and you can leave your hand 5 inches above the fire for 2 to 3 seconds, the coals are ready.

Sprinkle both sides of the burgers with the salt and pepper. Place the burgers on the grate and grill until well seared on both sides, about 5 minutes for medium rare or 6 minutes for medium. Transfer to buns or a serving platter and serve immediately with additional caramelized onions.

Alternatively, place a cast iron skillet over high heat and when it is hot but not smoking add the burgers to the dry pan. Cook until well seared on both sides, 8 to 10 minutes for medium rare or 10 to 12 minutes for medium.

Asian Beef Burgers with Ginger and Cilantro

Reminiscent of a favorite grilled steak from a local Chinese restaurant, this burger is for ginger lovers. Do not substitute dried ginger for the fresh: unless you are baking, dried ginger rarely works.

1½ to 1¾ pounds ground chuck

¼ cup chopped cilantro leaves

4 garlic cloves, minced

1 heaping tablespoon finely chopped
   fresh gingerroot

1 tablespoon hot sesame oil, available at
   Asian markets and specialty shops

1 teaspoon kosher salt

Place the beef, cilantro, garlic, ginger and sesame oil in a large mixing bowl and, using your hands, gently mix until the ingredients are evenly incorporated.

Place the beef on a work surface and divide into 4 balls of equal size. Form each into a patty about ¾ to 1 inch thick, tossing it back and forth between your hands. To ensure more even cooking, make a ½-inch indentation with your thumb in the center of the burger. Handle the patties as little as possible; do not work more than necessary.

Prepare a grill to medium-high. When the coals are glowing red, after 15 to 20 minutes, cover with the grate. After 5 minutes, use a wire brush to thoroughly clean the grate. Brush the grate with oil. When the coals are covered with pale gray ash and you can leave your hand 5 inches above the fire for 2 to 3 seconds, the coals are ready.

Sprinkle both sides of the burgers with the salt. Place the burgers on the grate and grill until well seared on both sides, about 5 minutes for medium rare or 6 minutes for medium. Transfer to buns or a serving platter on greens and serve immediately.

Alternatively, place a cast iron skillet over high heat and when it is hot but not smoking add the burgers to the dry pan. Cook until well seared on both sides, 8 to 10 minutes for medium rare or 10 to 12 minutes for medium.

Beef Burgers with Soy and Lemon

Very subtle in flavoring, the soy sauce in these burgers makes them slightly reminiscent of Asian foods.

1½ to 1¾ pounds ground chuck

4 scallions, both white and green parts, minced

3 tablespoons soy sauce, plus additional
   for serving

1 heaping tablespoon grated lemon zest

½ teaspoon kosher salt

½ teaspoon freshly ground black pepper

1 lemon, quartered

Place the beef, scallions, soy sauce and lemon zest in a large mixing bowl and, using your hands, gently mix until the ingredients are evenly incorporated.

Place the beef on a work surface and divide into 4 balls of equal size. Form each into a patty about ¾ to 1 inch thick, tossing it back and forth between your hands. To ensure more even cooking, make a ½-inch indentation with your thumb in the center of the burger. Handle the patties as little as possible; do not work more than necessary.

Prepare a grill to medium-high. When the coals are glowing red, after 15 to 20 minutes, cover with the grate. After 5 minutes, use a wire brush to thoroughly clean the grate. Brush the grate with oil. When the coals are covered with pale gray ash and you can leave your hand 5 inches above the fire for 2 to 3 seconds, the coals are ready.

Sprinkle both sides of the burgers with the salt and pepper. Place the burgers on the grate and grill until well seared on both sides, about 5 minutes for medium rare or 6 minutes for medium. Transfer to a serving platter and serve immediately with the lemon wedges and extra soy sauce.

Alternatively, place a cast iron skillet over high heat and when it is hot but not smoking add the burgers to the dry pan. Cook until well seared on both sides, 8 to 10 minutes for medium rare or 10 to 12 minutes for medium.

Mozzarella, Canadian Bacon and Grilled Pineapple Burgers

MAKES 4 BURGERS

Inspired by a pizza I used to order when I was in college, this burger boasts the great contrast of meaty and rich with fruity and light.

1½ to 1¾ pounds ground chuck

3 ounces mozzarella, chopped

3 ounces Canadian bacon, cooked and crumbled

1 teaspoon kosher salt

½ to 1 teaspoon freshly ground black pepper

Four ¼-inch-thick slices fresh pineapple

Place the beef on a work surface and divide into 4 balls of equal size. Divide the mozzarella cheese into 4 portions of equal size. Using your thumb or the back of a tablespoon, make a shallow hole in each portion of beef and fill it with cheese. Add a quarter of the bacon to each. Shape the burger and carefully seal the opening. Form each into a patty about ¾ to 1 inch thick, tossing it back and forth between your hands. To ensure more even cooking, make a ½-inch indentation with your thumb in the center of the burger. Handle the patties as little as possible; do not work more than necessary.

Prepare a grill to medium-high. When the coals are glowing red, after 15 to 20 minutes, cover with the grate. After 5 minutes, use a wire brush to thoroughly clean the grate. Brush the grate with oil. When the coals are covered with pale gray ash and you can leave your hand 5 inches above the fire for 2 to 3 seconds, the coals are ready.

Sprinkle both sides of the burgers with the salt and pepper. Place the burgers on the grate and grill until well seared on both sides, about 5 minutes for medium rare or 6 minutes for medium. When you are ready to turn the burgers, place the pineapple slices on the grill and cook about 2 minutes per side. Transfer the burgers to a serving platter, top with grilled pineapple and serve immediately.

Alternatively, place a cast iron skillet over high heat and when it is hot but not smoking add the burgers to the dry pan. Cook until well seared on both sides, 8 to 10 minutes for medium rare or 10 to 12 minutes for medium.

Portobello Burger

My friend Susan Benett taught me how to cook a better portobello mushroom: remove the black insides. Without them, the mushroom stays drier (instead of waterlogged) and better able to hold ingredients. This burger is perfect for the mushroom lover who doesn't want all the carbohydrates found in bread. This calls for making an open-faced burger, but you can cook another four mushroom caps and place them on top, if desired.

Olive oil, for the pan

4 portobello caps, stem and gills removed

2 cups baby arugula

8 thin slices tomato

¼ pound smoked mozzarella cheese,
  thinly sliced

1 teaspoon kosher salt

½ teaspoon freshly ground
  black pepper

Preheat the oven to 400°F. Lightly oil a baking sheet.

Place the portobello caps on the baking sheet and roast for 10 minutes. Transfer the baking sheet to a heatproof surface. Top each mushroom with ½ cup arugula, 2 slices tomato and a quarter of the cheese. Sprinkle with the salt and pepper. Return to the oven and roast until the arugula wilts and the cheese melts, about 5 minutes. Serve immediately.

Dijon Tuna Burger

Whatever you do, do not use a food processor to cut the tuna. You want it to be chopped, not ground!

1½ pounds yellowfin tuna, finely chopped by hand

2 tablespoons Dijon mustard

2 tablespoons finely chopped fresh basil leaves

2 garlic cloves, minced

2 teaspoons finely chopped fresh gingerroot

½ teaspoon cayenne pepper

2 tablespoons all purpose flour

1 teaspoon kosher salt

2 tablespoons olive oil

1 lime, quartered

Red onion rings and greens, for serving (optional)

Place the tuna, mustard, basil, garlic, ginger and pepper in a large mixing bowl and toss gently to combine.

Place the flour and salt on a large plate. Divide the tuna mixture into 4 patties and dredge them in the mixture. Cover and refrigerate for at least 30 minutes and up to 8 hours.

Place a large skillet over medium-high heat and when it is hot, add the oil. Add the patties and cook until rare on the inside and well browned on the outside, 3 to 4 minutes on each side. Serve immediately, garnished with the lime quarters and red onion rings and greens, if desired.

Espresso Rubbed Burgers

MAKES 4 BURGERS

These are not burgers for buns. Instead, serve them with lemon wedges: as with a cup of espresso, the tartness of the lemon brings out the flavor of the bitter coffee. Either way, it will be impossible for dinner guests to guess the mysterious ingredient in this rub.

1 tablespoon plus 1 teaspoon coarsely ground espresso beans

2 teaspoons kosher salt

1 to 2 teaspoons coarse freshly ground black pepper

1 teaspoon brown sugar

1 teaspoon chili powder

½ teaspoon ground cinnamon

1½ to 1¾ pounds ground chuck

1 lemon, quartered

Place the ground espresso, salt, pepper, brown sugar, chili powder and cinnamon on a large plate and mix well.

Place the beef on a work surface and divide into 4 balls of equal size. Dredge the balls in the espresso mixture and form each into a patty about ¾ to 1 inch thick, tossing it back and forth between your hands. To ensure more even cooking, make a ½-inch indentation with your thumb in the center of the burger. Handle the patties as little as possible; do not work more than necessary.

Place a cast iron skillet over high heat and when it is hot but not smoking add the burgers to the dry pan. Cook until well seared on both sides, 8 to 10 minutes for medium rare or 10 to 12 minutes for medium. Serve immediately, garnished with the lemon quarters.

Caramelized Onions
and Blue Cheese Burgers

MAKES 4 BURGERS

Caramelizing onions takes a bit of time but the end result is sweet, rich and sensuous. Like Roasted Garlic (page 48), having some on hand can make a good dish even better (and certainly less time consuming). Feel free to substitute goat cheese or mozzarella cheese for the blue cheese.

FOR THE CARAMELIZED ONIONS:

2 tablespoons olive oil

2 large red, Spanish or sweet onions, thinly sliced

2 garlic cloves, minced or thinly sliced (optional)

1 tablespoon fresh rosemary leaves

½ teaspoon kosher salt, or more to taste

FOR THE BURGERS:

1½ to 1¾ pounds ground chuck

3 ounces blue cheese, crumbled, plus extra
   for topping

1 teaspoon kosher salt

½ to 1 teaspoon freshly ground black pepper

To make the caramelized onions: Place a large skillet over low heat and when it is hot, add the oil. Add the remaining ingredients and cook, stirring only occasionally as necessary, until the onions are deeply browned and slightly gooey, about 40 minutes. If the onions dry out, add water, 1 tablespoon at a time. Use immediately or cover and refrigerate for up to 2 days. (Yield: ¾ to 1 cup)

To make the burgers: Place the beef on a work surface and divide into 4 balls of equal size. Divide the blue cheese into 4 portions of equal size. Using your thumb or the back of a tablespoon, make a shallow hole in each portion of beef and fill it with the blue cheese. Shape the burger and carefully seal the opening. Form each into a patty about ¾ to 1 inch thick, tossing it back and forth between your hands. To ensure more even cooking, make a ½-inch indentation with your thumb in the center of the burger. Handle the patties as little as possible; do not work more than necessary.

Prepare a grill to medium-high. When the coals are glowing red, after 15 to 20 minutes, cover with the grate. After 5 minutes, use a wire brush to thoroughly clean the

grate. Brush the grate with oil. When the coals are covered with pale gray ash and you can leave your hand 5 inches above the fire for 2 to 3 seconds, the coals are ready.

Sprinkle both sides of the burgers with the salt and pepper. Place the burgers on the grate and grill until well seared on both sides, about 5 minutes for medium rare or 6 minutes for medium. Top with a few crumbles of cheese and let melt, if desired. Transfer to buns (or toast as shown) or a serving platter and serve immediately.

Alternatively, place a cast iron skillet over high heat and when it is hot but not smoking add the burgers to the dry pan. Cook until well seared on both sides, 8 to 10 minutes for medium rare or 10 to 12 minutes for medium.

Spicy Beef Burgers with Apricots and Prunes

MAKES 4 BURGERS

Although this combination may seem completely bizarre, it is, in fact, completely delicious and takes its root from slow simmered meat dishes, like beef stew and brisket. Don't be tempted to leave out the flour from the fruits: it allows them to stay separate and not clump together.

½ cup chopped dried apricots

½ cup chopped dried prunes

1 teaspoon all purpose flour

1½ to 1¾ pounds ground chuck

4 scallions, both white and green parts, minced

2 garlic cloves or 4 caramelized garlic cloves (page 9), finely chopped

2 teaspoons Vietnamese chili paste

1 teaspoon kosher salt

½ to 1 teaspoon freshly ground black pepper

Place the apricots, prunes and flour in a large bowl and toss until the fruits are well covered with flour and don't stick to each other. Add the beef, scallions, garlic and chili paste and, using your hands, mix until the ingredients are evenly incorporated. Place the mixture on a work surface and divide into 4 balls of equal size. Form each into a patty about ¾ to 1 inch thick, tossing it back and forth between your hands. To ensure more even cooking, make a ½-inch indentation with your thumb in the center of the burger. Handle the patties as little as possible; do not work more than necessary.

Prepare a grill to medium-high. When the coals are glowing red, after 15 to 20 minutes, cover with the grate. After 5 minutes, use a wire brush to thoroughly clean the grate. Brush the grate with oil. When the coals are covered with pale gray ash and you can leave your hand 5 inches above the fire for 2 to 3 seconds, the coals are ready.

Sprinkle both sides of the burgers with the salt and pepper. Place the burgers on the grate and grill until well seared on both sides, about 5 minutes for medium rare or 6 minutes for medium. Transfer to buns or a serving platter and serve immediately.

Alternatively, place a cast iron skillet over high heat and when it is hot but not smoking add the burgers to the dry pan. Cook until well seared on both sides, 8 to 10 minutes for medium rare or 10 to 12 minutes for medium.

Turkey Burgers with Indian Spices

My friends seem to either love or hate cumin—with its bitter, pungent, warm but slightly dusty flavor. Its not one of those spices you can just slip in. Mostly used in the spicier foods of Mexican, Indian and Cuban cuisines, it is generally known as an ingredient in curry powder and in chili.

1¼ to 1½ pounds ground turkey (1 package)

4 garlic cloves, minced

2 tablespoons minced fresh gingerroot

Juice and grated zest of 1 lime

1½ teaspoons ground cumin

1½ teaspoons freshly ground black pepper

1½ teaspoons ground cinnamon

½ teaspoon ground cardamom

1½ teaspoons kosher salt

1 lime, quartered

Place the turkey, garlic, ginger, lime juice and zest, cumin, pepper, cinnamon and cardamom in a bowl and, using your hands, mix until the ingredients are evenly incorporated. Place the mixture on a work surface and divide into 4 balls of equal size. Form each into a patty about ¾ to 1 inch thick, tossing it back and forth between your hands. Handle the patties as little as possible; do not work more than necessary.

Prepare a grill to medium-high. When the coals are glowing red, after 15 to 20 minutes, cover with the grate. After 5 minutes, use a wire brush to thoroughly clean the grate. Brush the grate with oil. When the coals are covered with pale gray ash and you can leave your hand 5 inches above the fire for 2 to 3 seconds, the coals are ready.

Sprinkle both sides of the burgers with the salt. Place the burgers on the grate and grill until well seared on both sides, about 5 minutes for medium rare or 6 minutes for medium. Transfer to buns or a serving platter and serve immediately with the lime quarters.

Alternatively, place a cast iron skillet over high heat and when it is hot but not smoking add the burgers to the dry pan. Cook until well seared on both sides, 8 to 10 minutes for medium rare or 10 to 12 minutes for medium.

Chris Jolly's Cheeseburger Club

MAKES 4 BURGERS

My friend Chris Jolly is as opinionated, passionate and adamant about his burgers as a person can be. This is one of his favorites, the one he makes when he is running the kitchen.

1½ to 1¾ pounds ground chuck

1 teaspoon kosher salt

½ teaspoon freshly ground black pepper

8 thin slices cheddar cheese

12 slices good quality white bread

¼ cup mayonnaise

8 slices cooked bacon

8 slices tomato

4 romaine leaves

Place the beef on a work surface and divide into 4 balls of equal size. Form each into a patty about ¾ to 1 inch thick, tossing it back and forth between your hands. To ensure more even cooking, make a ½-inch indentation with your thumb in the center of the burger. Handle the patties as little as possible; do not work more than necessary.

Prepare a grill to medium-high. When the coals are glowing red, after 15 to 20 minutes, cover with the grate. After 5 minutes, use a wire brush to thoroughly clean the grate. Brush the grate with oil. When the coals are covered with pale gray ash and you can leave your hand 5 inches above the fire for 2 to 3 seconds, the coals are ready.

Sprinkle both sides of the burgers with the salt and pepper. Place the burgers on the grate and grill until well seared on both sides, about 5 minutes for medium rare or 6 minutes for medium. A minute or two before the burger is done, top each with 2 slices of the cheddar cheese and let melt.

Alternatively, place a cast iron skillet over high heat and when it is hot but not smoking add the burgers to the dry pan. Cook until well seared on both sides, 8 to 10 minutes for medium rare or 10 to 12 minutes for medium.

continued on page 37

Place the finished cheeseburger on a slice of white bread. Top with another slice of bread. Spread 1 tablespoon of mayonnaise on each slice. Top each with 2 slices bacon, 2 slices tomato and 1 leaf romaine lettuce. Top with another slice of white bread. Cut each sandwich in half and serve immediately.

Spicy Chipotle Turkey Burgers

Wrinkled and dark brown in color, canned chipotles are readily available in adobo sauce: a thick liquid of tomato, vinegar and spice. They are surprisingly versatile and impart a smoky sweet and warm flavor.

1¼ to 1½ pounds ground turkey (1 package)

2 to 3 garlic cloves, minced

1 canned chipotle chiles in adobo, chopped

2 teaspoons dried oregano

1 teaspoon Dijon mustard

1 teaspoon chili powder

1 teaspoon ground cumin

⅛ to ¼ teaspoon cayenne (optional)

1 teaspoon kosher salt

½ teaspoon freshly ground black pepper

Place the turkey, garlic, chipotles, oregano, mustard, chili powder, cumin and cayenne, if desired, in a bowl and, using your hands, mix until the ingredients are evenly incorporated. Place the mixture on a work surface and divide into 4 balls of equal size. Form each into a patty about ¾ to 1 inch thick, tossing it back and forth between your hands. Handle the patties as little as possible; do not work more than necessary.

Prepare a grill to medium-high. When the coals are glowing red, after 15 to 20 minutes, cover with the grate. After 5 minutes, use a wire brush to thoroughly clean the grate. Brush the grate with oil. When the coals are covered with pale gray ash and you can leave your hand 5 inches above the fire for 2 to 3 seconds, the coals are ready.

Sprinkle both sides of the burgers with the salt and pepper. Place the burgers on the grate and grill until well seared on both sides, about 5 minutes for medium rare or 6 minutes for medium. Transfer to buns or a serving platter and serve immediately.

Alternatively, place a cast iron skillet over high heat and when it is hot but not smoking add the burgers to the dry pan. Cook until well seared on both sides, 8 to 10 minutes for medium rare or 10 to 12 minutes for medium.

Lamb Burgers with Hoisin and Scallions

MAKES 4 BURGERS

Lamb burgers with a decidedly Chinese twist, these are great served on a bed of steamed rice. Hoisin, a sweet spicy Chinese sauce made from fermented soybeans, garlic, vinegar and peppers, and also known as Peking sauce, is usually used in very small amounts as a condiment or glaze.

1½ to 1¾ pounds ground lamb	1 tablespoon soy sauce
2 tablespoons hoisin sauce	1 teaspoon crushed red pepper flakes
4 scallions, both white and green parts, chopped	1 garlic clove, finely chopped
2 tablespoons chopped fresh cilantro leaves	1 teaspoon kosher salt
2 tablespoons chopped fresh mint leaves	½ teaspoon freshly ground black pepper
1 tablespoon finely chopped fresh gingerroot	1 lime, quartered

Place the lamb, hoisin, scallions, cilantro, mint, ginger, soy sauce, red pepper flakes and garlic in a large bowl and, using your hands, mix until the ingredients are evenly incorporated. Place the mixture on a work surface and divide into 4 balls of equal size. Form each into a patty about ¾ to 1 inch thick, tossing it back and forth between your hands. Handle the patties as little as possible; do not work more than necessary.

Prepare a grill to medium-high. When the coals are glowing red, after 15 to 20 minutes, cover with the grate. After 5 minutes, use a wire brush to thoroughly clean the grate. Brush the grate with oil. When the coals are covered with pale gray ash and you can leave your hand 5 inches above the fire for 2 to 3 seconds, the coals are ready.

Sprinkle both sides of the burgers with the salt and pepper. Place the burgers on the grate and grill until well seared on both sides, about 4 minutes for medium rare or 5 minutes for medium. Transfer to a serving platter and serve immediately with the lime quarters.

Alternatively, place a cast iron skillet over high heat and when it is hot but not smoking add the burgers to the dry pan. Cook until well seared on both sides, 8 to 10 minutes for medium rare or 10 to 12 minutes for medium.

Spicy Black Bean Burgers

A little bit like a black bean taco, these burgers are spot-on when accompanied by lettuce, tomato, guacamole, salsa, jack cheese and sour cream.

4 cups cooked, rinsed and drained
   black beans

½ cup panko breadcrumbs

2 large eggs

4 scallions, both white and green parts, minced

3 tablespoons chopped basil or cilantro,
   or a combination

2 garlic cloves, minced

1½ to 2 teaspoons ground cumin

1½ teaspoons dried oregano

1 to 2 teaspoons crushed red pepper flakes

1 teaspoon kosher salt

½ teaspoon freshly ground black pepper

Place 2 cups of the black beans in the bowl of a food processor fitted with a steel blade and pulse until chunky. Transfer to a large mixing bowl, add the remaining whole black beans, along with the panko, eggs, scallions, basil or cilantro, garlic, cumin, oregano, and red pepper flakes and mix until well combined.

Divide the mixture into 4 portions and form each into a patty about ¾ to 1 inch thick, tossing it back and forth between your hands. Sprinkle the patties with the salt and pepper. Place a cast iron skillet over high heat and when it is hot but not smoking add the burgers to the dry pan. Cook until well seared on both sides and heated throughout, 8 to 10 minutes. Serve immediately.

Chipotle and Scallion Burgers

Chipotles, ripened and smoked jalapeño peppers, are readily available at grocery and specialty shops and add a wonderful smoky spicy element that I love. Keep a few cans in your pantry.

1½ to 1¾ pounds ground chuck

3 garlic cloves, finely chopped

2 tablespoons minced scallions, both white and green parts

1 tablespoon minced canned chipotle chile in adobo

1 teaspoon kosher salt

½ teaspoon freshly ground black pepper

1 lime, quartered

Place the beef, garlic, scallions and chipotle in a large bowl and, using your hands, mix until the ingredients are evenly incorporated. Place the mixture on a work surface and divide into 4 balls of equal size. Form each into a patty about ¾ to 1 inch thick, tossing it back and forth between your hands. To ensure more even cooking, make a ½-inch indentation with your thumb in the center of the burger. Handle the patties as little as possible; do not work more than necessary.

Prepare a grill to medium-high. When the coals are glowing red, after 15 to 20 minutes, cover with the grate. After 5 minutes, use a wire brush to thoroughly clean the grate. Brush the grate with oil. When the coals are covered with pale gray ash and you can leave your hand 5 inches above the fire for 2 to 3 seconds, the coals are ready.

Sprinkle both sides of the burgers with the salt and pepper. Place the burgers on the grate and grill until well seared on both sides, about 5 minutes for medium rare or 6 minutes for medium. Transfer to buns or a serving platter and serve immediately with the lime quarters.

Alternatively, place a cast iron skillet over high heat and when it is hot but not smoking add the burgers to the dry pan. Cook until well seared on both sides, 8 to 10 minutes for medium rare or 10 to 12 minutes for medium.

Turkey Burgers with Feta and Herbs

This combination—mint, rosemary, parsley and oregano—is decidedly Greek, which is why I stuffed the inside with feta cheese. Serve it with a salad of chopped tomatoes and cucumbers. It's one of my summertime favorites.

1¼ to 1½ pounds ground turkey (1 package)

3 tablespoons chopped fresh mint leaves

2 tablespoons chopped fresh rosemary

2 tablespoons chopped fresh Italian flat leaf parsley leaves

2 garlic cloves, minced

2 teaspoons dried oregano

1 teaspoon Dijon mustard

¼ to ½ teaspoon freshly ground black pepper

⅛ to ¼ teaspoon cayenne (optional)

4 tablespoons feta cheese

1 teaspoon kosher salt

½ teaspoon freshly ground black pepper

1 lemon, quartered

Place the turkey, mint, rosemary, parsley, garlic, oregano, mustard, pepper and cayenne, if desired, in a large bowl and, using your hands, mix until the ingredients are evenly incorporated. Place the mixture on a work surface and divide into 4 balls of equal size. Divide the feta cheese into 4 portions of equal size. Using your thumb or the back of a tablespoon, make a shallow hole in each portion of beef and fill it with cheese. Shape the burger and carefully seal the opening. Form each into a patty about ¾ to 1 inch thick, tossing it back and forth between your hands. Handle the patties as little as possible; do not work more than necessary.

Prepare a grill to medium-high. When the coals are glowing red, after 15 to 20 minutes, cover with the grate. After 5 minutes, use a wire brush to thoroughly clean the grate. Brush the grate with oil. When the coals are covered with pale gray ash and you can leave your hand 5 inches above the fire for 2 to 3 seconds, the coals are ready.

continued on page 45

43

Sprinkle both sides of the burgers with the salt and pepper. Place the burgers on the grate and grill until well seared on both sides, about 5 minutes for medium rare or 6 minutes for medium. Transfer to buns, pita pockets or a serving platter and serve immediately with the lemon quarters.

Alternatively, place a cast iron skillet over high heat and when it is hot but not smoking add the burgers to the dry pan. Cook until well seared on both sides, 8 to 10 minutes for medium rare or 10 to 12 minutes for medium.

Spinach and Feta Cheese Burgers

It wasn't until after I ate this burger that it occurred to me that it had all the classic ingredients of spanakopita, a savory Greek pie-like combination of phyllo dough filled with spinach, feta cheese and herbs. The combination works really well with the beef.

1½ to 1¾ pounds ground chuck

1 cup chopped flat leaf spinach, plus extra for serving

½ cup chopped feta cheese

2 garlic cloves, finely minced

1 teaspoon chopped fresh rosemary leaves

½ teaspoon fresh oregano, plus extra for garnish, or 1 teaspoon dried oregano

1 teaspoon kosher salt

½ teaspoon freshly ground black pepper

1 lemon, quartered

Place the beef, spinach, feta cheese, garlic, rosemary and oregano in a large mixing bowl and, using your hands, gently mix until the ingredients are evenly incorporated.

Place the beef on a work surface and divide into 4 balls of equal size. Form each into a patty about ¾ to 1 inch thick, tossing it back and forth between your hands. To ensure more even cooking, make a ½-inch indentation with your thumb in the center of the burger. Handle the patties as little as possible; do not work more than necessary.

Prepare a grill to medium-high. When the coals are glowing red, after 15 to 20 minutes, cover with the grate. After 5 minutes, use a wire brush to thoroughly clean the grate. Brush the grate with oil. When the coals are covered with pale gray ash and you can leave your hand 5 inches above the fire for 2 to 3 seconds, the coals are ready.

Sprinkle both sides of the burgers with the salt and pepper. Place the burgers on the grate and grill until well seared on both sides, about 5 minutes for medium rare or 6 minutes for medium. Transfer to a serving platter and serve immediately with fresh spinach leaves, fresh oregano and the lemon quarters.

Alternatively, place a cast iron skillet over high heat and when it is hot but not smoking add the burgers to the dry pan. Cook until well seared on both sides, 8 to 10 minutes for medium rare or 10 to 12 minutes for medium.

Roasted Garlic Burgers with Guacamole

It's hard to imagine what food isn't improved by the addition of guacamole or roasted garlic (well, maybe not ice cream, although...). I suggest keeping roasted garlic in your fridge all the time: it's incredibly easy to make but if you don't have some on hand, it can feel like a chore. It adds a depth and richness that raw or even sautéed garlic doesn't. Serve these burgers with tortilla chips.

FOR THE ROASTED GARLIC:

1 head garlic

1 tablespoon olive oil

¼ teaspoon kosher salt

FOR THE GUACAMOLE:

2 perfectly ripe avocados, coarsely chopped

¼ cup coarsely chopped tomato

2 scallions, both white and green parts, chopped

3 tablespoons chopped fresh cilantro leaves

¼ teaspoon cayenne pepper

¼ teaspoon kosher salt

¼ teaspoon crushed red pepper flakes

1 tablespoon freshly squeezed lime juice

1 teaspoon finely minced jalapeño pepper
    or chipotle chile (optional)

FOR THE BURGERS:

1½ to 1¾ pounds ground chuck

1 teaspoon kosher salt

½ to 1 teaspoon freshly ground black pepper

To make the roasted garlic: Preheat the oven to 450°F. Remove as much of the paper from the garlic as possible, being careful to keep the head intact. Rub with the oil and sprinkle with the salt. Place on a large piece of aluminum foil and then seal the aluminum foil so that it forms a packet. Place in the oven and cook until the garlic is soft and tender, about 45 minutes. When cool enough to handle, remove the peel, and mash the cloves with a fork. Use immediately or cover and refrigerate up to 5 days.

To make the guacamole: Place all the ingredients in a bowl and mash gently to mix. Use immediately or cover and refrigerate up to 4 hours.

To make the burgers: Place the beef on a work surface, add the mashed garlic and mix together. Divide into 4 balls of equal size. Form each into a patty about ¾ to 1 inch thick, tossing it back and forth between your hands. To ensure more even cooking, make a ½-inch indentation with your thumb in the center of the burger. Handle the patties as little as possible; do not work more than necessary.

Prepare a grill to medium-high. When the coals are glowing red, after 15 to 20 minutes, cover with the grate. After 5 minutes, use a wire brush to thoroughly clean the grate. Brush the grate with oil. When the coals are covered with pale gray ash and you can leave your hand 5 inches above the fire for 2 to 3 seconds, the coals are ready.

Sprinkle both sides of the burgers with the salt and pepper. Place the burgers on the grate and grill until well seared on both sides, about 5 minutes for medium rare or 6 minutes for medium. Transfer to buns or a serving platter and serve immediately, topped with guacamole.

Alternatively, place a cast iron skillet over high heat and when it is hot but not smoking add the burgers to the dry pan. Cook until well seared on both sides, 8 to 10 minutes for medium rare or 10 to 12 minutes for medium.

Harissa Rubbed Burgers

Harissa is an often fiery Tunisian sauce made from generous amounts of chile peppers, garlic, spices and sometimes tomatoes. Mostly used as a condiment, it is often paired with couscous, served with pasta and sandwiches and as a rub for meat, which inspired its use here. Substituting red pepper flakes isn't exactly authentic but even so, delicious and necessary for a rub.

2½ teaspoons ground cumin

2 teaspoons paprika

2 teaspoons kosher salt

1 teaspoon cayenne pepper

1 teaspoon crushed red pepper flakes

1 teaspoon garlic powder

1 teaspoon caraway seeds

1¼ to 1½ pounds ground turkey or chicken
  (1 package)

Place the cumin, paprika, salt, cayenne, red pepper flakes, garlic powder and caraway seeds on a large plate and mix well.

Place the ground turkey on a work surface and divide into 4 balls of equal size. Dredge the balls in the cumin mixture and form each into a patty about ¾ to 1 inch thick, tossing it back and forth between your hands. Handle the patties as little as possible; do not work more than necessary.

Place a cast iron skillet over high heat and when it is hot but not smoking add the burgers to the dry pan. Cook until well seared on both sides, 8 to 10 minutes for medium rare or 10 to 12 minutes for medium. Transfer to buns or a serving platter and serve immediately with ketchup.

Alternatively, prepare a grill to medium-high. When the coals are glowing red, after 15 to 20 minutes, cover with the grate. After 5 minutes, use a wire brush to thoroughly clean the grate. Brush the grate with oil. When the coals are covered with pale gray ash and you can leave your hand 5 inches above the fire for 2 to 3 seconds, the coals are ready.

Place the burgers on the grate and grill until well seared on both sides, 8 to 10 minutes for medium rare or 10 to 12 minutes for medium.

Mushroom Turkey Burgers

Although this burger doesn't have to be made with portobello mushrooms, their meatiness adds a nice body to the ground turkey. Feel free to substitute shiitakes, cremini or even button mushrooms.

1¼ to 1½ pounds ground turkey or chicken (1 package)

2 cups chopped brown (baby portobello) mushrooms

3 tablespoons chopped fresh mint leaves

3 tablespoons chopped fresh chives

3 garlic cloves, minced

1 teaspoon kosher salt

½ teaspoon freshly ground black pepper

Place the turkey, mushrooms, mint, chives and garlic in a large bowl and, using your hands, mix until the ingredients are evenly incorporated. Place the mixture on a work surface and divide into 4 balls of equal size. Form each into a patty about ¾ to 1 inch thick, tossing it back and forth between your hands. Handle the patties as little as possible; do not work more than necessary.

Prepare a grill to medium-high. When the coals are glowing red, after 15 to 20 minutes, cover with the grate. After 5 minutes, use a wire brush to thoroughly clean the grate. Brush the grate with oil. When the coals are covered with pale gray ash and you can leave your hand 5 inches above the fire for 2 to 3 seconds, the coals are ready.

Sprinkle both sides of the burgers with the salt and pepper. Place the burgers on the grate and grill until well seared on both sides, about 5 minutes for medium rare or 6 minutes for medium. Transfer to buns or a serving platter and serve immediately.

Alternatively, place a cast iron skillet over high heat and when it is hot but not smoking add the burgers to the dry pan. Cook until well seared on both sides, 8 to 10 minutes for medium rare or 10 to 12 minutes for medium.

Bacon and Cheddar Burgers

MAKES 4 BURGERS

Here is your basic burger elevated by stuffing—instead of topping—with the double whammy of bacon and cheese. You can select almost any cheese: my favorites include blue cheese and feta but you can also use mozzarella, Monterey Jack, Brie, Gouda or if you must, American.

1½ to 1¾ pounds ground chuck

4 ounces aged cheddar cheese, diced

8 slices cooked bacon, crumbled, plus extra
   bacon for serving (optional)

1 teaspoon kosher salt

½ to 1 teaspoon freshly ground
   black pepper

Place the beef on a work surface and divide into 4 balls of equal size. Divide the cheddar cheese and bacon into 4 portions of equal size. Using your thumb or the back of a tablespoon, make a shallow hole in each portion of beef and fill it with cheese. Add a quarter of the bacon to each burger. Shape the burger and carefully seal the opening. Form each into a patty about ¾ to 1 inch thick, tossing it back and forth between your hands. To ensure more even cooking, make a ½-inch indentation with your thumb in the center of the burger. Handle the patties as little as possible; do not work more than necessary.

Prepare a grill to medium-high. When the coals are glowing red, after 15 to 20 minutes, cover with the grate. After 5 minutes, use a wire brush to thoroughly clean the grate. Brush the grate with oil. When the coals are covered with pale gray ash and you can leave your hand 5 inches above the fire for 2 to 3 seconds, the coals are ready.

Sprinkle both sides of the burgers with the salt and pepper. Place the burgers on the grate and grill until well seared on both sides, about 5 minutes for medium rare or 6 minutes for medium. Transfer to buns or a serving platter and serve immediately, topped with bacon, if desired.

Alternatively, place a cast iron skillet over high heat and when it is hot but not smoking add the burgers to the dry pan. Cook until well seared on both sides, 8 to 10 minutes for medium rare or 10 to 12 minutes for medium.

Chicken Diablo Burgers with Roasted Red Peppers

Diablo sauce usually refers to a spicy red pepper, garlic, basil and oregano sauce found on pasta and shrimp.

FOR THE ROASTED PEPPERS:

3 red bell peppers

FOR THE BURGERS:

1¼ to 1½ pounds ground chicken or turkey
   (1 package)

¼ cup chopped fresh basil leaves, plus extra
   leaves for serving (optional)

3 garlic cloves, minced

2 teaspoons crushed red pepper flakes

1 teaspoon dried oregano

1 teaspoon kosher salt

½ teaspoon freshly ground black
   pepper

To make the roasted peppers: Preheat the broiler. Cut off the top and the bottom of each pepper so that you have a short column-like thing. Then slit the pepper open and discard the seeds. Flatten it out so that it resembles a small piece of paper.

Place the peppers, shiny side up, directly under broiler, as close together as possible, and cook until charred all over. While still hot, remove the peppers and place in a heavy plastic or paper bag, close shut and let sweat for about 10 minutes. Scrape off and discard the burned skin. Set aside to cool. Cut into strips, cover and refrigerate for up to 3 weeks.

To make the burgers: Place the chicken, basil, garlic, red pepper flakes and oregano in a large bowl and, using your hands, mix until the ingredients are evenly incorporated. Place the mixture on a work surface and divide into 4 balls of equal size. Form each into a patty about ¾ to 1 inch thick, tossing it back and forth between your hands. To ensure more even cooking, make a ½-inch indentation with your thumb in the center of the burger. Handle the patties as little as possible; do not work more than necessary.

continued on page 56

Prepare a grill to medium-high. When the coals are glowing red, after 15 to 20 minutes, cover with the grate. After 5 minutes, use a wire brush to thoroughly clean the grate. Brush the grate with oil. When the coals are covered with pale gray ash and you can leave your hand 5 inches above the fire for 2 to 3 seconds, the coals are ready.

Sprinkle both sides of the burgers with the salt and pepper. Place the burgers on the grate and grill until well seared on both sides, about 5 minutes for medium rare or 6 minutes for medium. Transfer to buns or a serving platter and serve immediately topped with the roasted peppers and with extra whole basil leaves, if desired.

Alternatively, place a cast iron skillet over high heat and when it is hot but not smoking add the burgers to the dry pan. Cook until well seared on both sides, 8 to 10 minutes for medium rare or 10 to 12 minutes for medium.

Burgers with Goat Cheese and Herbes de Provence

Herbes de Provence, a readily available blend of savory, rosemary, cracked fennel, thyme, basil, tarragon, lavender and marjoram, makes this easy burger taste like lots of work, which it—fortunately—isn't.

¾ cup goat or feta cheese, crumbled

2 tablespoons herbes de Provence

1½ to 1¾ pounds ground chuck

1½ teaspoons kosher salt

¾ teaspoon freshly ground black pepper

Place the goat cheese and herbes de Provence in a small mixing bowl and mix to combine.

Place the beef on a work surface and divide into 4 balls of equal size. Divide the cheese mixture into 4 portions of equal size. Using your thumb or the back of a tablespoon, make a shallow hole in each portion of beef and fill it with cheese. Shape the burger and carefully seal the opening. Form each into a patty about ¾ to 1 inch thick, tossing it back and forth between your hands. To ensure more even cooking, make a ½-inch indentation with your thumb in the center of the burger. Handle the patties as little as possible; do not work more than necessary.

Prepare a grill to medium-high. When the coals are glowing red, after 15 to 20 minutes, cover with the grate. After 5 minutes, use a wire brush to thoroughly clean the grate. Brush the grate with oil. When the coals are covered with pale gray ash and you can leave your hand 5 inches above the fire for 2 to 3 seconds, the coals are ready.

Sprinkle both sides of the burgers with the salt and pepper. Place the burgers on the grate and grill until well seared on both sides, about 5 minutes for medium rare or 6 minutes for medium. Transfer to a serving platter and serve immediately.

Alternatively, place a cast iron skillet over high heat and when it is hot but not smoking add the burgers to the dry pan. Cook until well seared on both sides, 8 to 10 minutes for medium rare or 10 to 12 minutes for medium.

Lamb Burgers with Herbs

Instead of serving these with ketchup try thickening some yogurt by leaving it overnight in cheesecloth.

FOR THE THICKENED YOGURT:

Muslin or cheesecloth

2 cups low fat or full fat plain yogurt

FOR THE BURGERS:

1½ to 1¾ pounds ground lamb

¼ cup chopped fresh mint leaves

¼ cup chopped fresh basil leaves

1 tablespoon chopped fresh rosemary

2 teaspoons dried fennel

1 teaspoon kosher salt

½ teaspoon freshly ground black pepper

1 lemon, quartered (optional)

To make the yogurt: Line a colander with muslin or cheesecloth. Place the colander over a large mixing bowl. Place the yogurt in the colander, cover and refrigerate for at least 4 hours and up to overnight. Discard the liquid in the bowl. Transfer the yogurt cheese to a small mixing bowl and use immediately or cover and refrigerate up to 4 days. (Yield: 2 cups)

To make the burgers: Place the lamb, mint, basil, rosemary and fennel in a large bowl and, using your hands, mix until the ingredients are evenly incorporated. Place the mixture on a work surface and divide into 4 balls of equal size. Form each into a patty about ¾ to 1 inch thick, tossing it back and forth between your hands. To ensure more even cooking, make a ½-inch indentation with your thumb in the center of the burger. Handle the patties as little as possible; do not work more than necessary.

Prepare a grill to medium-high. When the coals are glowing red, after 15 to 20 minutes, cover with the grate. After 5 minutes, use a wire brush to thoroughly clean the grate. Brush the grate with oil. When the coals are covered with pale gray ash and you can leave your hand 5 inches above the fire for 2 to 3 seconds, the coals are ready.

continued on page 60

Sprinkle both sides of the burgers with the salt and pepper. Place the burgers on the grate and grill until well seared on both sides, about 4 minutes for medium rare or 5 minutes for medium. Transfer to pita bread pockets or a serving platter and serve immediately with yogurt and/or lemon quarters.

Alternatively, place a cast iron skillet over high heat and when it is hot but not smoking add the burgers to the dry pan. Cook until well seared on both sides, 8 to 10 minutes for medium rare or 10 to 12 minutes for medium.

Pizza Burgers

Last Valentine's Day we had a huge snowstorm and my son Ben was craving pizza. I didn't really want him to brave the snow to get it but wanted to make him happy. My solution: a burger with all the typical pizza fixin's.

1½ to 1¾ pounds ground chuck

½ cup freshly grated Parmesan cheese

¼ cup chopped fresh basil leaves
  (about 10 leaves)

¼ cup tomato paste

1 tablespoon dried oregano

2 garlic cloves or 4 caramelized garlic cloves
  (page 9), finely chopped

⅓ cup shredded mozzarella

1 teaspoon kosher salt

½ to 1 teaspoon freshly ground black pepper

Place the beef, Parmesan cheese, basil, tomato paste, oregano and garlic in a large bowl and, using your hands, mix until the ingredients are evenly incorporated. Place the mixture on a work surface and divide into 4 balls of equal size. Divide the mozzarella into 4 balls of equal size. Using your thumb or the back of a tablespoon, make a shallow hole in each portion of beef and fill it with cheese. Shape the burger and carefully seal the opening. Form each into a patty about ¾ to 1 inch thick, tossing it back and forth between your hands. To ensure more even cooking, make a ½-inch indentation with your thumb in the center of the burger. Handle the patties as little as possible; do not work more than necessary.

Prepare a grill to medium-high. When the coals are glowing red, after 15 to 20 minutes, cover with the grate. After 5 minutes, use a wire brush to thoroughly clean the grate. Brush the grate with oil. When the coals are covered with pale gray ash and you can leave your hand 5 inches above the fire for 2 to 3 seconds, the coals are ready.

Sprinkle both sides of the burgers with the salt and pepper. Place the burgers on the grate and grill until well seared on both sides, about 5 minutes for medium rare or 6 minutes for medium. Transfer to buns or a serving platter and serve immediately.

Alternatively, place a cast iron skillet over high heat and when it is hot but not smoking add the burgers to the dry pan. Cook until well seared on both sides, 8 to 10 minutes for medium rare or 10 to 12 minutes for medium.

BURGERS

61

Beef Burgers with Feta, Cucumber, Avocado and Tomatoes

Basically a burger with a Greek salad on top.

½ cup crumbled feta cheese	1 tablespoon olive oil
½ English cucumber, diced	Juice of 1 lemon
1 perfectly ripe avocado, diced	1½ to 1¾ pounds ground chuck
1 beefsteak tomato, cored and diced	1 teaspoon kosher salt
1 tablespoon fresh oregano leaves	½ to 1 teaspoon freshly ground black pepper

Place the feta, cucumber, avocado, tomato, oregano, olive oil and lemon juice in a small bowl and mix to combine. Set aside.

Place the beef on a work surface and divide into 4 balls of equal size. Form each into a patty about ¾ to 1 inch thick, tossing it back and forth between your hands. To ensure more even cooking, make a ½-inch indentation with your thumb in the center of the burger. Handle the patties as little as possible; do not work more than necessary.

Prepare a grill to medium-high. When the coals are glowing red, after 15 to 20 minutes, cover with the grate. After 5 minutes, use a wire brush to thoroughly clean the grate. Brush the grate with oil. When the coals are covered with pale gray ash and you can leave your hand 5 inches above the fire for 2 to 3 seconds, the coals are ready.

Sprinkle both sides of the burgers with the salt and pepper. Place the burgers on the grate and grill until well seared on both sides, about 5 minutes for medium rare or 6 minutes for medium. Transfer to buns or a serving platter and serve immediately topped with equal amounts of the feta mixture.

Alternatively, place a cast iron skillet over high heat and when it is hot but not smoking add the burgers to the dry pan. Cook until well seared on both sides, 8 to 10 minutes for medium rare or 10 to 12 minutes for medium.

Beef Burgers with Jalapeños and Basil

It wasn't until I made this burger that I fell in love with jalapeños. I have always preferred chipotles, their smoky counterpart, but after discovering this burger, I find I am slicing up jalapeños to put on sandwiches and in salads and omelets. Don't be alarmed at the large quantity in this recipe: the beef seems to calm down the heat. On the other hand, feel free to reduce the amount.

1½ to 1¾ pounds ground chuck

4 garlic cloves, finely minced

¼ cup chopped jalapeño peppers (yes, this is right)

¼ cup chopped fresh basil leaves

2 tablespoons balsamic vinegar

1 teaspoon Kosher salt

½ to 1 teaspoon freshly ground black pepper

1 lime, quartered

Place the beef, garlic, jalapeños, basil and balsamic vinegar in a large mixing bowl and, using your hands, gently mix until the ingredients are evenly incorporated. Place the mixture on a work surface and divide into 4 balls of equal size. Form each into a patty about ¾ to 1 inch thick, tossing it back and forth between your hands. To ensure more even cooking, make a ½-inch indentation with your thumb in the center of the burger. Handle the patties as little as possible; do not work more than necessary.

Prepare a grill to medium-high. When the coals are glowing red, after 15 to 20 minutes, cover with the grate. After 5 minutes, use a wire brush to thoroughly clean the grate. Brush the grate with oil. When the coals are covered with pale gray ash and you can leave your hand 5 inches above the fire for 2 to 3 seconds, the coals are ready.

Sprinkle both sides of the burgers with the salt and pepper. Place the burgers on the grate and grill until well seared on both sides, about 5 minutes for medium rare or 6 minutes for medium. Transfer to buns or a serving platter and serve immediately with the lime quarters.

Alternatively, place a cast iron skillet over high heat and when it is hot but not smoking add the burgers to the dry pan. Cook until well seared on both sides, 8 to 10 minutes for medium rare or 10 to 12 minutes for medium.

Luther Burgers

There is almost no recipe in existence that is less like me than a Luther Burger, but I couldn't resist including this bizarre recipe in this book, which is, after all, supposed to be an exhaustive treatise on burgers. Legend has it that the late R&B artist Luther Vandross invented this burger, another that he merely loved it. Sometimes it's served as described below and sometimes with bacon (five slices per burger) and cheese. It's not for the faint of heart, literally.

1½ pounds ground chuck

1 teaspoon kosher salt

½ to 1 teaspoon freshly ground black pepper

2 tablespoons vegetable oil

4 donuts, split in half

Place the beef on a work surface and divide into 4 balls of equal size. Form each into a patty about 1 inch thick, tossing it back and forth between your hands. To ensure more even cooking, make a ½-inch indentation with your thumb in the center of the burger. Handle the patties as little as possible; do not work more than necessary. Sprinkle the burgers with the salt and pepper.

Place a cast iron skillet over high heat and when it is hot but not smoking, add the oil. Add the donuts, cut side down, and cook until lightly toasted. Remove from the pan and transfer to a platter.

Add the burgers and cook until well seared on both sides, 8 to 10 minutes for medium rare or 10 to 12 minutes for medium. Remove the burgers and place between two donuts halves, cut side on the outside. Return the now donut encased burgers to the pan and cook for an additional minute on each side. Transfer to a platter and serve immediately.

Cuban Style Pork Burger

Instead of adding the more commonly used lime zest for this group of flavors, I substituted grapefruit zest as a necessity and found when I later went back to the traditional combination that I preferred grapefruit!

1½ to 1¾ pounds ground pork

¼ cup chopped fresh cilantro leaves, plus extra
    for garnish

2 garlic cloves or 4 caramelized garlic cloves
    (page 9), finely chopped

1 heaping tablespoon dried oregano

1 tablespoon freshly grated grapefruit zest

2 teaspoons ground cumin

1 teaspoon kosher salt

½ to 1 teaspoon freshly ground black pepper

Place the pork, cilantro, garlic, oregano, grapefruit zest and cumin in a large bowl and, using your hands, mix until the ingredients are evenly incorporated. Place the mixture on a work surface and divide into 4 balls of equal size. Form each into a patty about ¾ to 1 inch thick, tossing it back and forth between your hands. To ensure more even cooking, make a ½-inch indentation with your thumb in the center of the burger. Handle the patties as little as possible; do not work more than necessary.

Prepare a grill to medium-high. When the coals are glowing red, after 15 to 20 minutes, cover with the grate. After 5 minutes, use a wire brush to thoroughly clean the grate. Brush the grate with oil. When the coals are covered with pale gray ash and you can leave your hand 5 inches above the fire for 2 to 3 seconds, the coals are ready.

Sprinkle both sides of the burgers with the salt and pepper. Place the burgers on the grate and grill until well seared on both sides, about 5 minutes for medium rare or 6 minutes for medium. Transfer to buns, small baguettes or a serving platter, garnish with cilantro and serve immediately.

Alternatively, place a cast iron skillet over high heat and when it is hot but not smoking add the burgers to the dry pan. Cook until well seared on both sides, 8 to 10 minutes for medium rare or 10 to 12 minutes for medium.

Barbecue Burgers

I often top my burgers with BBQ sauce instead of ketchup: here I put the BBQ ingredients directly into the burger. I like to serve these with a squeeze of lime juice but additional BBQ sauce is also an excellent addition.

6 scallions, both white and green parts, chopped	2 teaspoons light brown sugar
3 tablespoons tomato paste	2 teaspoons Dijon mustard
1 garlic clove or 2 caramelized garlic cloves (page 9), minced	1 teaspoon freshly ground black pepper
	1½ to 1¾ pounds ground chuck
1 tablespoon soy sauce	1 teaspoon kosher salt
1 tablespoon chili powder	1 lemon or lime, quartered
Grated zest of ½ lemon	

Place the scallions, tomato paste, garlic, soy sauce, chili powder, lemon zest, brown sugar, mustard and pepper in a large mixing bowl and mix until well combined. Add the beef and, using your hands, gently mix until the ingredients are evenly incorporated.

Place the beef on a work surface and divide into 4 balls of equal size. Form each into a patty about ¾ to 1 inch thick, tossing it back and forth between your hands. To ensure more even cooking, make a ½-inch indentation with your thumb in the center of the burger. Handle the patties as little as possible; do not work more than necessary.

Prepare a grill to medium-high. When the coals are glowing red, after 15 to 20 minutes, cover with the grate. After 5 minutes, use a wire brush to thoroughly clean the grate. Brush the grate with oil. When the coals are covered with pale gray ash and you can leave your hand 5 inches above the fire for 2 to 3 seconds, the coals are ready.

Sprinkle both sides of the burgers with the salt. Place the burgers on the grate and grill until well seared on both sides, about 5 minutes for medium rare or 6 minutes for medium. Transfer to buns or a serving platter and serve immediately, garnished with lemon quarters.

Alternatively, place a cast iron skillet over high heat and when it is hot but not smoking add the burgers to the dry pan. Cook until well seared on both sides, 8 to 10 minutes for medium rare or 10 to 12 minutes for medium.

Beef Burgers with Monterey Jack, Chiles, Bacon and Sour Cream

MAKES 4 BURGERS

Often called Jack cheese, the Jack in the name refers to David Jacks, the man who first marketed this mild semi-hard cheese. However, the Monterey in the name is from the Franciscan monks in Monterey, California, who made it. If you don't want the bother of chopping chiles, simply substitute Pepper Jack cheese.

1½ to 1¾ pounds ground chuck

8 slices bacon, cooked and crumbled, plus extra
    for serving (optional)

¼ cup finely chopped jalapeño pepper

¼ cup chopped fresh Italian flat leaf
    parsley leaves

4 scallions, both white and green parts, chopped,
    plus extra for serving (optional)

2 garlic cloves or 4 caramelized garlic cloves
    (page 9), finely chopped

¼ pound Monterey Jack cheese, diced

1 teaspoon kosher salt

½ to 1 teaspoon freshly ground
    black pepper

¼ cup sour cream

Place the beef, bacon, jalapeño, parsley, scallions and garlic in a large bowl and, using your hands, mix until the ingredients are evenly incorporated. Place the mixture on a work surface and divide into 4 balls of equal size. Divide the Monterey Jack into 4 portions of equal size. Using your thumb or the back of a tablespoon, make a shallow hole in each portion of beef and fill it with cheese. Shape the burger and carefully seal the opening. Form each into a patty about ¾ to 1 inch thick, tossing it back and forth between your hands. To ensure more even cooking, make a ½-inch indentation with your thumb in the center of the burger. Handle the patties as little as possible; do not work more than necessary.

Prepare a grill to medium-high. When the coals are glowing red, after 15 to 20 minutes, cover with the grate. After 5 minutes, use a wire brush to thoroughly clean the grate. Brush the grate with oil. When the coals are covered with pale gray ash and you can leave your hand 5 inches above the fire for 2 to 3 seconds, the coals are ready.

continued on page 72

Sprinkle both sides of the burgers with the salt and pepper. Place the burgers on the grate and grill until well seared on both sides, about 5 minutes for medium rare or 6 minutes for medium. Transfer to buns or a serving platter and serve immediately, garnished with the sour cream, plus extra bacon and scallions, if desired.

Alternatively, place a cast iron skillet over high heat and when it is hot but not smoking add the burgers to the dry pan. Cook until well seared on both sides, 8 to 10 minutes for medium rare or 10 to 12 minutes for medium.

Todd's Turkey Burgers

Todd English, the chef and owner of Olives restaurants (and more), invented this home recipe when he was looking for a high protein–low fat meal. His burger used hand chopped chicken and an egg white but I substituted ground turkey, making it easier and quicker while still as tasty.

1¼ to 1½ pounds ground turkey (1 package)

½ cup chopped fresh cilantro leaves

⅓ red onion, finely chopped

3 garlic cloves, finely chopped

1 tablespoon finely chopped fresh gingerroot

1 to 1½ teaspoons Vietnamese chili garlic sauce

1 teaspoon Dijon mustard

1 teaspoon kosher salt

1 teaspoon freshly ground black pepper

1 to 2 limes, quartered

Place the turkey, cilantro, onion, garlic, ginger, chili garlic sauce and mustard in a large bowl and, using your hands, mix until the ingredients are evenly incorporated. Place the mixture on a work surface and divide into 4 balls of equal size. Form each into a patty about ¾ to 1 inch thick, tossing it back and forth between your hands. Handle the patties as little as possible; do not work more than necessary.

Prepare a grill to medium-high. When the coals are glowing red, after 15 to 20 minutes, cover with the grate. After 5 minutes, use a wire brush to thoroughly clean the grate. Brush the grate with oil. When the coals are covered with pale gray ash and you can leave your hand 5 inches above the fire for 2 to 3 seconds, the coals are ready.

Sprinkle both sides of the burgers with the salt and pepper. Place the burgers on the grate and grill until well seared on both sides, about 5 minutes for medium rare or 6 minutes for medium. Transfer to buns or a serving platter and serve immediately with the lime quarters.

Alternatively, place a cast iron skillet over high heat and when it is hot but not smoking add the burgers to the dry pan. Cook until well seared on both sides, 8 to 10 minutes for medium rare or 10 to 12 minutes for medium.

Curried Cheddar Burgers with Chutney

Inspired by the English ploughman's lunch, a hunk of cheddar and sometimes a pickled vegetable or chutney, this is one of my very favorite combinations. It started out in my repertoire as a roast beef sandwich but transformed into this much adored burger.

1 tablespoon white sugar

2 teaspoons kosher salt

1½ tablespoons curry powder

½ teaspoon freshly ground black pepper

1½ to 1¾ pounds ground chuck

¾ cup coarsely shredded sharp cheddar cheese

⅓ cup mango chutney, plus additional for serving

1 lime, quartered

Place the sugar, salt, curry powder and pepper in a small mixing bowl and mix to combine.

Place the beef on a work surface and divide into 4 balls of equal size. Divide the cheese into 4 portions of equal size. Using your thumb or the back of a tablespoon, make a shallow hole in each portion of beef and fill it with cheese. Add a heaping tablespoon of chutney to each patty. Shape the burger and carefully seal the opening. Form each into a patty about ¾ to 1 inch thick, tossing it back and forth between your hands. To ensure more even cooking, make a ½-inch indentation with your thumb in the center of the burger. Handle the patties as little as possible; do not work more than necessary. Dredge the burgers in the curry mixture.

Prepare a grill to medium-high. When the coals are glowing red, after 15 to 20 minutes, cover with the grate. After 5 minutes, use a wire brush to thoroughly clean the grate. Brush the grate with oil. When the coals are covered with pale gray ash and you can leave your hand 5 inches above the fire for 2 to 3 seconds, the coals are ready.

Place the burgers on the grate and grill until well seared on both sides, about 5 minutes for medium rare or 6 minutes for medium. Transfer to a serving platter and serve immediately with chutney and the lime quarters.

Alternatively, place a cast iron skillet over high heat and when it is hot but not smoking add the burgers to the dry pan. Cook until well seared on both sides, 8 to 10 minutes for medium rare or 10 to 12 minutes for medium.

Sicilian Pork Burgers

Lusty, spicy and herby, these burgers are great served with sautéed eggplant, tomatoes and peppers dotted with lightly toasted pine nuts.

1½ to 1¾ pounds ground pork

¼ cup chopped fresh flat leaf parsley leaves

3 tablespoons chopped fresh rosemary leaves

1 heaping tablespoon finely chopped fresh
   mint leaves

2 garlic cloves or 4 caramelized garlic cloves
   (page 9), finely chopped

1 tablespoon plus 1 teaspoon tomato paste

1 teaspoon dried marjoram or oregano

1 teaspoon red pepper flakes

½ teaspoon dried sage

1 teaspoon kosher salt

½ to 1 teaspoon freshly ground
   black pepper

Place the pork, parsley, rosemary, mint, garlic, tomato paste, marjoram, pepper flakes and sage in a large bowl and, using your hands, mix until the ingredients are evenly incorporated. Place the mixture on a work surface and divide into 4 balls of equal size. Form each into a patty about ¾ to 1 inch thick, tossing it back and forth between your hands. Handle the patties as little as possible; do not work more than necessary.

Prepare a grill to medium-high. When the coals are glowing red, after 15 to 20 minutes, cover with the grate. After 5 minutes, use a wire brush to thoroughly clean the grate. Brush the grate with oil. When the coals are covered with pale gray ash and you can leave your hand 5 inches above the fire for 2 to 3 seconds, the coals are ready.

Sprinkle both sides of the burgers with the salt and pepper. Place the burgers on the grate and grill until well seared on both sides, about 5 minutes for medium rare or 6 minutes for medium. Transfer to buns or a serving platter and serve immediately.

Alternatively, place a cast iron skillet over high heat and when it is hot but not smoking add the burgers to the dry pan. Cook until well seared on both sides, 8 to 10 minutes for medium rare or 10 to 12 minutes for medium.

Salmon Burgers with Mint

If you haven't tried panko (Japanese breadcrumbs), you don't know what you are missing: lighter than American breadcrumbs and while most often used for frying, I especially like to use them in recipes where I need to bind ingredients together.

1½ pounds salmon fillet, chopped by hand

¾ cup panko breadcrumbs

2 shallots, minced

½ cup chopped fresh mint leaves

1 tablespoon fresh thyme leaves or 1 teaspoon dried thyme

1 teaspoon Dijon mustard

2 tablespoons mayonnaise

2 teaspoons freshly grated lemon zest

1 teaspoon kosher salt

½ to 1 teaspoon freshly ground black pepper

Place the salmon, breadcrumbs, shallots, mint, thyme, mustard, mayonnaise and lemon zest in a large bowl and, using your hands, mix until the ingredients are evenly incorporated. Place the mixture on a work surface and divide into 4 balls of equal size. Form each into a patty about ¾ to 1 inch thick, tossing it back and forth between your hands. Handle the patties as little as possible; do not work more than necessary.

Prepare a grill to medium-high. When the coals are glowing red, after 15 to 20 minutes, cover with the grate. After 5 minutes, use a wire brush to thoroughly clean the grate. Brush the grate with oil. When the coals are covered with pale gray ash and you can leave your hand 5 inches above the fire for 2 to 3 seconds, the coals are ready.

Sprinkle both sides of the burgers with the salt and pepper. Place the burgers on the grate and grill until well seared on both sides, about 5 minutes for medium rare or 6 minutes for medium. Transfer to buns or a serving platter and serve immediately.

Alternatively, place a cast iron skillet over high heat and when it is hot but not smoking add the burgers to the dry pan. Cook until well seared on both sides, 8 to 10 minutes for medium rare or 10 to 12 minutes for medium.

Chicken, Camembert and Cranberry Burgers

I have been preparing this spicy-sweet chunky cranberry chutney for years and years. It started out as a Thanksgiving fixture which then migrated to Christmas. I discovered that I loved it so much I eventually kept bags of cranberries in the freezer so I could always have it on hand. Delicious on chicken, turkey and beef burgers, it is also, not surprisingly, great on turkey and roast beef sandwiches. It's also great on a spoon.

FOR THE CRANBERRY CHUTNEY:

One 12-ounce bag cranberries (3 cups)

¼ cup orange juice

1 to 2 jalapeño peppers or chipotle chiles, minced

½ cup light brown sugar

¾ cup lightly toasted pecans or walnuts (see page 82), coarsely chopped

Grated zest of 1 lime

Grated zest of 1 orange

½ teaspoon kosher salt

FOR THE BURGERS:

1¼ to 1½ pounds ground chicken or turkey

4 ounces Camembert

1 teaspoon kosher salt

½ to 1 teaspoon freshly ground black pepper

To make the chutney: Place the cranberries, orange juice, jalapeño and sugar in a small saucepan and cook over medium-high heat until the cranberries are soft and have absorbed all the liquid, about 10 minutes. Set aside to cool.

Add the nuts, lime and orange zests and salt to the chutney and stir to combine. If not using immediately, cover and refrigerate for up to 2 weeks. (Yield: about 2 cups)

To make the burgers: Place the chicken on a work surface and divide into 4 balls of equal size. Divide the Camembert cheese into 4 portions of equal size. Using your thumb or the back of a tablespoon, make a shallow hole in each portion of beef and fill it with cheese. Shape the burger and carefully seal the opening. Form each into a patty about ¾ to 1 inch thick, tossing it back and forth between your hands. Handle the patties as little as possible; do not work more than necessary.

continued on page 82

Prepare a grill to medium-high. When the coals are glowing red, after 15 to 20 minutes, cover with the grate. After 5 minutes, use a wire brush to thoroughly clean the grate. Brush the grate with oil. When the coals are covered with pale gray ash and you can leave your hand 5 inches above the fire for 2 to 3 seconds, the coals are ready.

Sprinkle both sides of the burgers with the salt and pepper. Place the burgers on the grate and grill until well seared on both sides, about 5 minutes for medium rare or 6 minutes for medium. Transfer to buns or a serving platter and serve immediately with generous amounts of cranberry chutney.

Alternatively, place a cast iron skillet over high heat and when it is hot but not smoking add the burgers to the dry pan. Cook until well seared on both sides, 8 to 10 minutes for medium rare or 10 to 12 minutes for medium.

Toasted Nuts

Place the nuts on a baking sheet or shallow pan and toast in a preheated 350°F oven until lightly colored and fragrant, about 10 minutes. Set aside to cool.

Salmon Burgers with Wasabi

MAKES 4 BURGERS

Most people are familiar with wasabi as the hot, green paste that accompanies sushi. It can be purchased in small tubes in the Asian foods section of better supermarkets. Be careful not to stick your nose right up to it: wasabi is experienced as spicier to the nasal passages than in the mouth.

1½ pounds salmon fillet, chopped by hand

½ bunch scallions, both white and green
   parts, chopped

3 to 4 tablespoons chopped fresh cilantro
   or basil leaves

1 large egg, lightly beaten

2 tablespoons mayonnaise

1 tablespoon wasabi paste

3 tablespoons panko breadcrumbs

1 teaspoon kosher salt

2 tablespoons olive oil

1 lime, quartered

Place the salmon, scallions, cilantro, egg, mayonnaise and wasabi paste in a large mixing bowl and toss gently to combine. Place the panko and salt on a large plate and mix to combine. Divide the salmon mixture into 4 patties and dredge them in the panko mixture. Cover and refrigerate for at least 30 minutes and up to 8 hours.

Place a large skillet over medium-high heat and when it is hot, add the oil. Add the patties and cook until well browned, about 3 minutes on each side. Serve immediately garnished with the lime quarters.

Cod Burgers Reminiscent of Fish Tacos

MAKES 4 BURGERS

I was absolutely prepared not to like this as I am not a fan of white fish. You might wonder why I would then include such a recipe: I wanted to include everything I could think of and I wanted to be open-minded. Light, spicy and fresh, I absolutely loved these burgers. Serve with avocados, salsa, mayo or sour cream, shredded cabbage and chopped tomatoes.

1½ pounds cod or another firm white fish like fluke

¾ cup panko breadcrumbs

½ cup chopped fresh cilantro leaves

¼ cup finely chopped red onion

2 jalapeño peppers, chopped

2 garlic cloves, minced

2 tablespoons mayonnaise

¼ cup yellow stone-ground cornmeal

1 teaspoon kosher salt

½ teaspoon freshly ground black pepper

Place the cod, panko, cilantro, onion, jalapeño, garlic and mayonnaise in a large bowl and, using your hands, mix until the ingredients are evenly incorporated. Place the mixture on a work surface and divide into 4 balls of equal size. Form each into a patty about ¾ to 1 inch thick, tossing it back and forth between your hands. Handle the patties as little as possible; do not work more than necessary.

Place the cornmeal, salt and pepper on a large plate and mix to combine. Dredge each patty in the mixture, cover and refrigerate for at least 1 hour and up to 4.

Prepare a grill to medium-high. When the coals are glowing red, after 15 to 20 minutes, cover with the grate. After 5 minutes, use a wire brush to thoroughly clean the grate. Brush the grate with oil. When the coals are covered with pale gray ash and you can leave your hand 5 inches above the fire for 2 to 3 seconds, the coals are ready.

Place the burgers on the grate and grill until well seared on both sides, about 5 minutes for medium rare or 6 minutes for medium. Transfer to buns or a serving platter and serve immediately.

Alternatively, place a cast iron skillet over high heat and when it is hot but not smoking add the burgers to the dry pan. Cook until well seared on both sides, 8 to 10 minutes for medium rare or 10 to 12 minutes for medium.

Spicy Salsa Salmon Cakes

MAKES 4 BURGERS

You can use almost any kind of salsa for these burgers: mango and pineapple are especially good.

1½ pounds salmon fillet, finely chopped by hand

½ bunch scallions, both white and green parts, chopped

½ cup favorite salsa, plus additional for garnish

3 to 4 tablespoons chopped fresh cilantro leaves

1 large egg, lightly beaten

2 tablespoons mayonnaise

2 tablespoons Dijon mustard

¼ cup yellow stone-ground cornmeal

3 tablespoons all purpose flour

1 teaspoon kosher salt

2 tablespoons olive oil

1 lime, quartered

Place the salmon, scallions, salsa, cilantro, egg, mayonnaise and mustard in a large mixing bowl and toss gently to combine. Place the cornmeal, flour and salt on a large plate and mix to combine. Divide the salmon mixture into 4 patties and dredge them in the cornmeal mixture. Cover and refrigerate for at least 30 minutes and up to 8 hours.

Place a large skillet over medium-high heat and when it is hot, add the oil. Add the patties and cook until well browned, about 3 minutes on each side. Serve immediately garnished with the lime quarters and additional salsa.

Caramelized Onion and Chickpea Burgers

Serve these a little smaller than most other burgers: they are incredibly rich and filling. Try them on a bed of greens with lots and lots of lemon wedges and thickened yogurt (page 58).

2 cups canned chickpeas, rinsed, drained
   and mashed by hand

1 cup caramelized onions (page 29)

½ cup panko breadcrumbs

6 garlic cloves, minced

2 tablespoons chopped fresh cilantro leaves

2 tablespoons sesame tahini

2 tablespoons fresh lemon juice

1 tablespoon chopped fresh rosemary leaves

1 teaspoon kosher salt

½ teaspoon freshly ground black pepper

2 lemons, quartered

Place the chickpeas, onions, panko, garlic, cilantro, tahini, lemon juice and rosemary in a large mixing bowl and mix until well combined. Divide the mixture into 4 portions and form each into a patty about ¾ to 1 inch thick, tossing it back and forth between your hands. Cover and refrigerate for at least 4 hours and up to overnight.

Sprinkle the patties with the salt and pepper. Place a cast iron skillet over high heat and when it is hot but not smoking add the burgers to the dry pan. Cook until well seared on both sides and heated throughout, 8 to 10 minutes. Serve immediately, garnished with lemon quarters.

Protein Burger with Thousand Island Dressing

MAKES 4 BURGERS

I t took years for my childhood pal Lizzy Shaw to convince me to try an In-N-Out Burger, but as soon as I relented, I became a devotee. Now, every time I fly to California I stop by an In-N-Out Burger before I go to wherever I am really supposed to be.

I always order their protein burger (an item not even listed on their menu), which substitutes a piece of iceberg lettuce for the roll. I have on occasion ordered a Double Double Protein: two patties (albeit small ones) with cheese wrapped in lettuce. Though they serve ketchup, the burgers come with their own version of Thousand Island. Here is mine:

FOR THE THOUSAND ISLAND DRESSING:

1 cup mayonnaise

⅓ cup American style chili sauce (not the ethnic varieties) or cocktail sauce

1 tablespoon prepared horseradish

1 tablespoon Worcestershire sauce

1 tablespoon fresh lemon juice

FOR THE BURGERS:

1½ to 1¾ pounds ground chuck

1 teaspoon kosher salt

½ to 1 teaspoon freshly ground black pepper

Romaine lettuce leaves, for serving

To make the thousand island dressing: Place the mayonnaise, chili sauce, horseradish, Worcestershire sauce and lemon juice in a small bowl and mix to combine. Cover and refrigerate for at least 1 hour and up to 1 week. If the dressing separates, simply shake well. (Yield: about 1½ cups)

To make the burgers: Place the beef on a work surface and divide into 4 balls of equal size. Form each into a patty about ¾ to 1 inch thick, tossing it back and forth between your hands. To ensure more even cooking, make a ½-inch indentation with your thumb in the center of the burger. Handle the patties as little as possible; do not work more than necessary.

Prepare a grill to medium-high. When the coals are glowing red, after 15 to 20 minutes, cover with the grate. After 5 minutes, use a wire brush to thoroughly clean the grate. Brush the grate with oil. When the coals are covered with pale gray ash and you can leave your hand 5 inches above the fire for 2 to 3 seconds, the coals are ready.

Sprinkle both sides of the burgers with the salt and pepper. Place the burgers on the grate and grill until well seared on both sides, about 5 minutes for medium rare or 6 minutes for medium. Wrap each burger in romaine leaves and add about 1 tablespoon dressing inside.

Alternatively, place a cast iron skillet over high heat and when it is hot but not smoking add the burgers to the dry pan. Cook until well seared on both sides, 8 to 10 minutes for medium rare or 10 to 12 minutes for medium.

Lemon Pepper Burgers

When I was a child, my mother, so enamored of lemon pepper, used to carry a jar of it in her purse. She no longer carries it with her but she convinced me of its charm and usefulness. There is little that isn't improved by its addition. Of course my version substitutes fresh lemon zest for the dried, yielding a version to make my mom proud.

3 tablespoons coarsely ground black pepper

Grated zest of 2 lemons

1½ teaspoons kosher salt

1½ to 1¾ pounds ground chuck

1 lemon, quartered

Place the pepper, lemon zest and salt on a plate and mix to combine.

Place the beef on a work surface and divide into 4 balls of equal size. Form each into a patty about ¾ to 1 inch thick, tossing it back and forth between your hands. Dredge the patties in the lemon pepper mixture. To ensure more even cooking, make a ½-inch indentation with your thumb in the center of the burger. Handle the patties as little as possible; do not work more than necessary.

Place a large skillet over medium-high heat and when it is very hot, add the burgers, making sure to let the pan reheat between additions. Cook until well seared on both sides, 8 to 10 minutes for medium rare or 10 to 12 minutes for medium. Serve immediately, garnished with lemon quarters.

Alternatively, prepare a grill to medium-high. When the coals are glowing red, after 15 to 20 minutes, cover with the grate. After 5 minutes, use a wire brush to thoroughly clean the grate. Brush the grate with oil. When the coals are covered with pale gray ash and you can leave your hand 5 inches above the fire for 2 to 3 seconds, the coals are ready.

Place the burgers on the grate and grill until well seared on both sides, about 5 minutes for medium rare or 6 minutes for medium. Transfer to buns or a serving platter and serve immediately.

Blackened Blue Burgers

MAKES 4 BURGERS

In my house we call these Ted Burgers because our friend Ted Simonides, who is a pretty straight meat-and-potatoes guy—and thinks green is green, meaning broccoli is asparagus is parsley—absolutely loved these spicy, crusty, creamy burgers, to the shock of his entire family.

1½ teaspoons dried oregano

1½ teaspoons garlic powder

1½ teaspoons dried thyme

1½ teaspoons Hungarian paprika

1½ teaspoons kosher salt

1 teaspoon cayenne pepper

1 teaspoon freshly ground black pepper

1½ to 1¾ pounds ground chuck

½ pound blue cheese, crumbled or cut into
   4 equal pieces

Preheat the broiler.

Place the oregano, garlic powder, thyme, paprika, salt, cayenne and black pepper on a large plate and mix together.

Place the beef on a work surface and divide into 4 balls of equal size. Divide the cheese into 4 portions of equal size. Using your thumb or the back of a tablespoon, make a shallow well in each portion of beef and fill it with cheese. Form each into a patty about ¾ to 1 inch thick, tossing it back and forth between your hands. Handle the patties as little as possible; do not work more than necessary. Dredge the burgers in the oregano mixture.

Prepare a grill to medium-high. When the coals are glowing red, after 15 to 20 minutes, cover with the grate. After 5 minutes, use a wire brush to thoroughly clean the grate. Brush the grate with oil. When the coals are covered with pale gray ash and you can leave your hand 5 inches above the fire for 2 to 3 seconds, the coals are ready.

Place the burgers on the grate and grill until well seared on both sides, about 5 minutes for medium rare or 6 minutes for medium. Transfer to buns or a serving platter and serve immediately.

Alternatively, place a cast iron skillet over high heat and when it is hot but not smoking add the burgers to the dry pan. Cook until well seared on both sides, 8 to 10 minutes for medium rare or 10 to 12 minutes for medium.

BURGERS

RECIPE OF THE WEEK

BURGERS

Index